A Book of Thanks

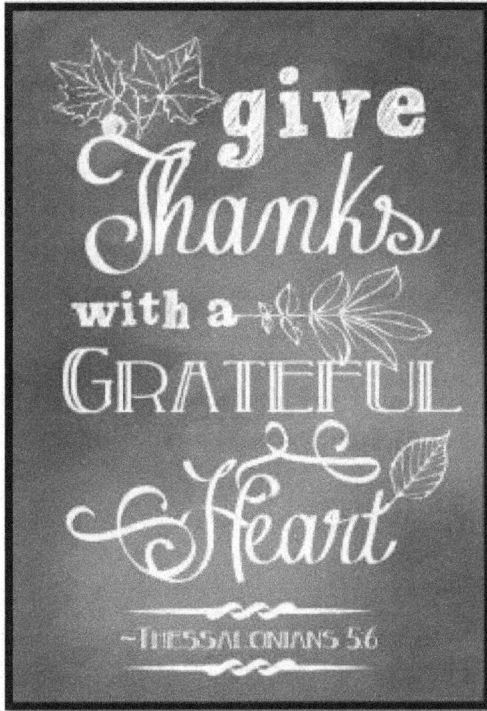

In everything give thanks;
for this is God's will for you in Christ Jesus.
I Thessalonians 5:18

Christmas, 2015

Dear Sisters and Brothers In Christ,

One of the earliest "cool" spiritual things I remember revolves around being thankful. I made an effort to see how long I could go if I tried to thank God each and every day for something *new*. Oh, I had the standard things I thanked God for, but I wondered how many days I could go thinking up something fresh to thank God for…a month? Maybe two?

It turned out to be a wonderful spiritual exercise. I remember over the course of a day I'd suddenly think, "Well, there's my new thankful thing for today!" or – even more surprising – "Wow, I didn't realize that I was supposed to be thankful for *that* when it happened two weeks ago!" In retrospect, I wish I had written my list down because I remember I went for what seemed a looooooooong time.

So here's my Christmas gift to you: <u>*A Book of Thanks*</u>. I started to make this just for myself and then I thought of you guys (you are all one of my "standard" thankfuls: *Every time I think of you, I give thanks to my God. Philippians 1:3.)*

Maybe, this time next year, we can share with each other some of our top thankfuls of the 2016 year and the blessings God continues to bring into our lives. Wouldn't that be fun?

The time of the Lord's favor has come. Luke 4:19

Because of our faith, Christ has brought us into this place of underserved privilege where we now stand, and we confidently and joyfully look forward to sharing God's glory. Romans 5:2

Love,

Sue XXOO

Table of Contents

The ABC's of My Prayers

I will praise the LORD at all times. I will constantly speak His praises. Psalm 31:1

       First things first: there are things that I pray for every day – people, concerns, world issues… It's my standard, go to prayer request list. Can you come up with one thing for every letter of the alphabet that you regularly pray for? It took me a while to compile a complete list but I was delighted with how wide ranging and yet pinpoint accurate my finished product finally turned out to be.

       (I even managed to come up with things for the hard letters although I stretched things a bit by praying for "X" for God to "x-ray my heart and see what I need to fix" and for "Z" I praise God for being the Alpha and Omega – the beginning and end of everything. Remember, there are really 'no rules' but the ones you choose to impose on yourself!)

A	
B	
C	
D	

E	
F	
G	
H	
I	
J	
K	
L	
M	

The ABC's of My Prayers

N	
O	
P	
Q	
R	
S	
T	
U	
V	

The ABC's of My Prayers

W	
X	
Y	
Z	

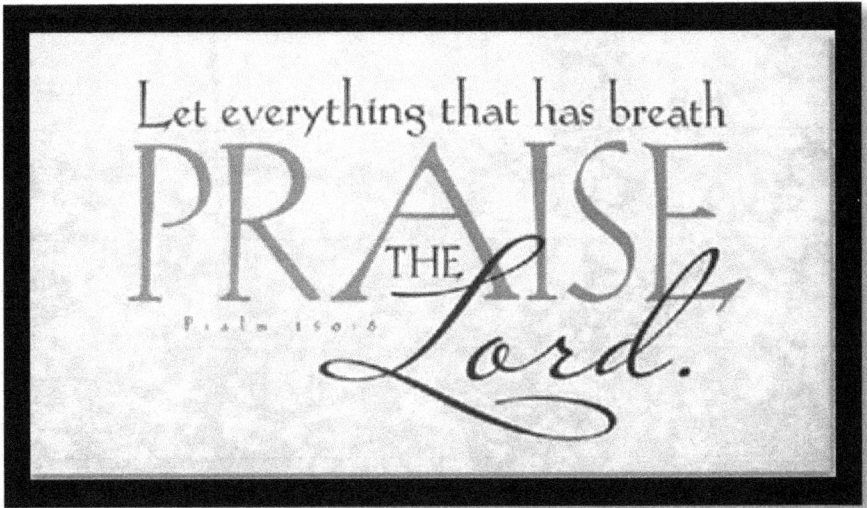

The ABC's of My Prayers

January

O give thanks to the Lord, for He is good, for
His steadfast love endures forever!
Psalm 107:1

1	
2	
3	
4	
5	
6	
7	
8	
9	
10	

January

11	
12	
13	
14	
15	
16	
17	
18	
19	
20	
21	
22	

January

23	
24	
25	
26	
27	
28	
29	
30	
31	

January

567
Wealth untold
Every
What the Lord has done
God is over
Doubt
Angels will attend
789
will fly
Count your many blessings
ALL
Helpant comfort
Name them
678
heaven
ONE by ONE
456
123
as The Days go by
Journeys eNd
Reward in

January

February

O give thanks to the Lord; for He is good; for
His mercy endures forever.
Psalm 136:1

1	
2	
3	
4	
5	
6	
7	
8	
9	
10	

February

11	
12	
13	
14	
15	
16	
17	
18	
19	
20	
21	
22	

February

23	
24	
25	
26	
27	
28	
29	

February

And let the peace of God rule in your hearts, to the which also ye are called in one body; and be ye thankful.
Colossians 3: 15

February

March

Giving thanks always and for everything to God the Father in the name of our Lord Jesus Christ. Ephesians 5:20

1	
2	
3	
4	
5	
6	
7	
8	
9	
10	

11	
12	
13	
14	
15	
16	
17	
18	
19	
20	
21	
22	

March

23	
24	
25	
26	
27	
28	
29	
30	
31	

March

It is not happy people who are thankful;

It is thankful people who are happy.

March

April

Every good gift and every perfect gift is from above, coming down from the Father of lights with whom there is no variation or shadow due to change. James 1:17

1	
2	
3	
4	
5	
6	
7	
8	
9	

10	
11	
12	
13	
14	
15	
16	
17	
18	
19	
20	
21	

April

22	
23	
24	
25	
26	
27	
28	
29	
30	

April

Living a Thankful Life

April

May

Do not be anxious about anything, but in everything by prayer and supplication with thanksgiving let your request be made known to God. Philippians 4:6

1	
2	
3	
4	
5	
6	
7	
8	
9	

May

10	
11	
12	
13	
14	
15	
16	
17	
18	
19	
20	
21	

May

22	
23	
24	
25	
26	
27	
28	
29	
30	
31	

May

THANKFULNESS IS THE SOIL
IN WHICH JOY THRIVES.

May

June

Thanks be to God for His inexpressible gift!
2 Corinthians 9:15

1	
2	
3	
4	
5	
6	
7	
8	
9	
10	

June

11	
12	
13	
14	
15	
16	
17	
18	
19	
20	
21	
22	

June

23	
24	
25	
26	
27	
28	
29	
30	

June

GIVE *Thanks* to the LORD FOR HE is Good
for His steadfast love endures forever

June

July

Praise the Lord! Oh give thanks to the Lord, for He is good, for His steadfast love endures forever! Psalm 106:1

1	
2	
3	
4	
5	
6	
7	
8	
9	
10	

July

11	
12	
13	
14	
15	
16	
17	
18	
19	
20	
21	
22	

July

23	
24	
25	
26	
27	
28	
29	
30	
31	

July

Piglet noticed that even though he had a very small heart, it could hold a rather large amount of Gratitude.
-A.A. Milne

July

August

Oh Give thanks to the Lord; call upon His name; make known His deeds among the peoples! Psalm 105:1

1	
2	
3	
4	
5	
6	
7	
8	
9	
10	

August

11	
12	
13	
14	
15	
16	
17	
18	
19	
20	
21	
22	

August

23	
24	
25	
26	
27	
28	
29	
30	
31	

August

GRATITUDE IS THE HEART'S MEMORY.

—FRENCH PROVERB

August

September

This is the day which the Lord has made;
we will rejoice and be glad in it.
Psalm 118:24

1	
2	
3	
4	
5	
6	
7	
8	
9	
10	

September

11	
12	
13	
14	
15	
16	
17	
18	
19	
20	
21	
22	

September

23	
24	
25	
26	
27	
28	
29	
30	

September

September

October

Since we are receiving a Kingdom that is unshakable, let us be thankful and please God by worshiping him with holy fear and awe. Hebrews 12:28

1	
2	
3	
4	
5	
6	
7	
8	
9	

October

10	
11	
12	
13	
14	
15	
16	
17	
18	
19	
20	
21	

October

22	
23	
24	
25	
26	
27	
28	
29	
30	
31	

October

COUNT YOUR MANY BLESSINGS NAME THEM ONE BY ONE COUNT YOUR MANY BLESSINGS SEE WHAT GOD HAS DONE

October

November

And now, just as you accepted Christ Jesus as your Lord, you must continue to follow him. Let your roots grow down into him, and let your lives be built on him. Then your faith will grow strong in the truth you were taught, and you will overflow with thankfulness. Colossians 2:6-7

1	
2	
3	
4	
5	
6	
7	
8	

November

9	
10	
11	
12	
13	
14	
15	
16	
17	
18	
19	
20	

November

21	
22	
23	
24	
25	
26	
27	
28	
29	
30	

November

✝

I have a lot to be thankful for.

December

The Lord is my strength and my shield; my heart trusts in Him, and I am helped. Therefore my heart exults. And with my song I shall thank Him. Psalm 28:7

1	
2	
3	
4	
5	
6	
7	
8	
9	

December

10	
11	
12	
13	
14	
15	
16	
17	
18	
19	
20	
21	

December

22	
23	
24	
25	
26	
27	
28	
29	
30	
31	

December

in
Everything,
always give
thanks.

December

The Year In Review

The Top Ten Things I am thankful for this year:

1.

2.

3.

4.

5.

6.

7.

8.

9.

10.

My greatest sources of joy this past year:

One thing that I wasn't thankful for at first but turned out to be a blessing in the end:

The top five people who have made the greatest spiritual impact on my life:

1.

2.

3.

4.

5.

My greatest source of unhappiness this year was:

What are some things I can do for next year that will help me deal with this big source of unhappiness in my life?

One surprising thing I discovered about myself this year as a result of doing *A Book of Thanks:*

For I know the
Plans
I have for you,
DECLARES THE LORD

Plans for
Hope and a *Future.*

Jeremiah 29:11

The Year In Review

www.ingramcontent.com/pod-product-compliance
Lightning Source LLC
Chambersburg PA
CBHW020608030426
42337CB00013B/1271